First published by Brockhampton Press Ltd
20 Bloomsbury Street
London WC1B 3QA

© Brockhampton Press Ltd. 1997
© Lys de Bray (all illustrations), 1997

ISBN 1 86019 111 8

Conceived and designed by Savitri Books Ltd.
Printed in Hong Kong by
South China Printing Company (1988) Limited

The wonderful illustrations in this Daybook come from a book
by Lys de Bray, entitled *Fantastic Garlands*, which was originally
published in 1982. The quotations were also selected
by the author from *The Temple Shakespeare*,
Cambridge edition (Dent, 1895).

ELIZABETHAN GARLANDS

– DAYBOOK –

Illustrated by
LYS DE BRAY

BROCKHAMPTON PRESS

JANUARY

*The count is neither sad, nor sick, nor
merry, nor well; but civil count, civil as an
orange, and something of that jealous complexion.*
Beatrice – *Much Ado About Nothing*

•

*. . . let them say of me, 'As jealous as Ford, that
searched a hollow walnut for his wife's leman.'*
Ford – *The Merry Wives of Windsor*

•

1

2

3

4

5

6

7

8

9

. . . to take note how many pair of silk
stockings thou hast, viz. these, and those that were
thy peach-coloured ones!
Prince Hal – *Henry IV*

10

11

Witness this primrose bank whereon I lie;
Venus and Adonis

12

13

14

15

16

17

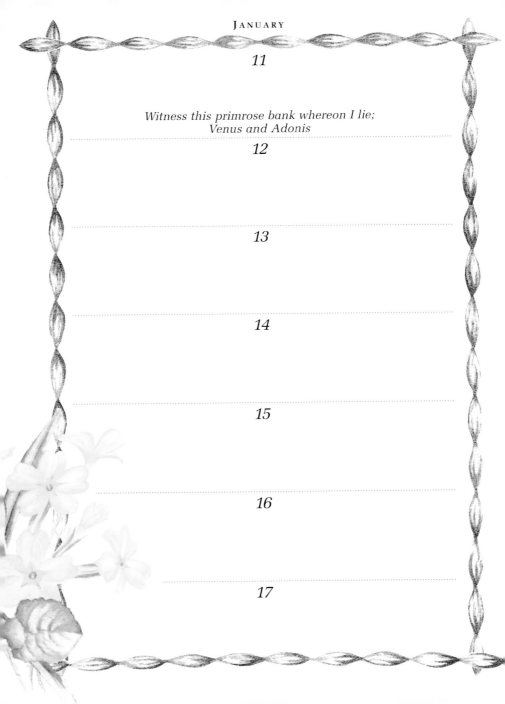

18

. . . weaving on their heads
garlands of bays . . .
The vision – *Henry V*

19

20

21

22

23

24

25

. . . bold oxlips and
The crown-imperial;
Perdita – *The Winter's Tale*

26

27

28

29

30

31

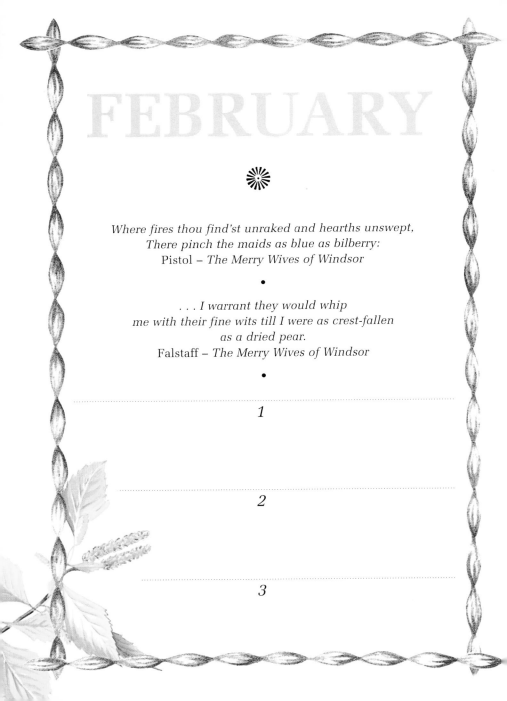

FEBRUARY

Where fires thou find'st unraked and hearths unswept,
There pinch the maids as blue as bilberry:
Pistol – *The Merry Wives of Windsor*

•

. . . I warrant they would whip
me with their fine wits till I were as crest-fallen
as a dried pear.
Falstaff – *The Merry Wives of Windsor*

•

1

2

3

4

The rank of osiers by the murmuring stream
Left on your right hand, brings you to the place
Celia – *As You Like It*

5

6

7

8

9

10

11

. . . so I charm'd their ears,
That, calf-like, they my lowing follow'd through
Tooth'd briers, sharp furzes, pricking goss, and thorns,
Which enter'd their frail shins:
Ariel – *The Tempest*

12

13

14

15

16

17

18

*There with fantastic garlands did she come
Of crow-flowers, nettles, daisies, and long purples,
That liberal shepherds give a grosser name,
But our cold maids do dead men's fingers call them:*
Gertrude – Hamlet

19

20

21

22

23

24

25

26

27

28/29

Notes

. . . and thy broom-groves,
Whose shadow the dismissed bachelor loves,
Being lass-lorn:
Iris – *The Tempest*

MARCH

Elinor: Come to thy grandam, child.
Constance: Do, child, go to it grandam, child;
Give grandam kingdom, and it grandam will
Give it a plum, a cherry, and a fig:
King John

•

Feed him with apricocks and dewberries,
Titania – *A Midsummer Night's Dream*

•

1

2

3

4

....

5

....

6

....

7

....

8

....

9

....

10

A purple flower sprung up, chequer'd with white,
Venus and Adonis

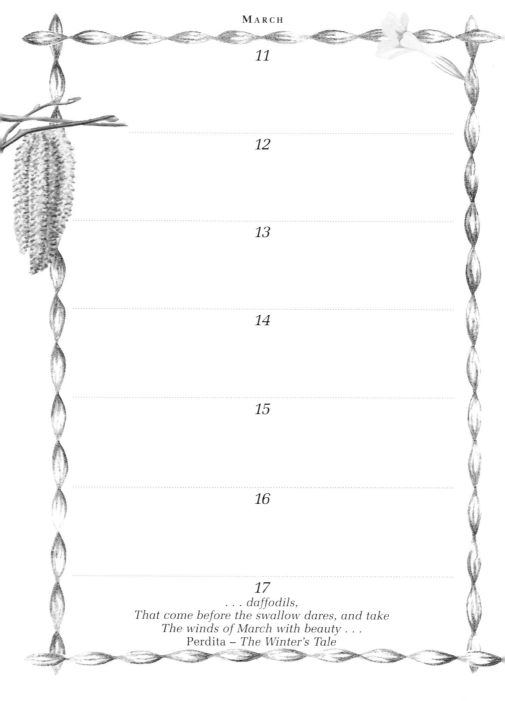

11

12

13

14

15

16

17

. . . daffodils,
That come before the swallow dares, and take
The winds of March with beauty . . .
Perdita – *The Winter's Tale*

18

With words more sweet, and yet more dangerous,
Then baits to fish, or honey-stalks to sheep;
Tamora – *Titus Andronicus*

19

20

21

22

23

24

25

26

27

28

29

30

31

When daisies pied and violets blue
And lady-smocks all silver-white . . .
Do paint the meadows with delight,
Armado – *Love's Labour's Lost*

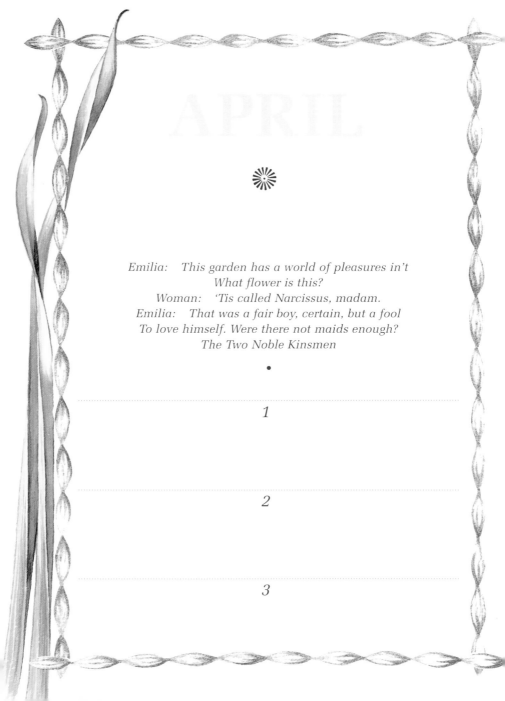

APRIL

Emilia: This garden has a world of pleasures in't
What flower is this?
Woman: 'Tis called Narcissus, madam.
Emilia: That was a fair boy, certain, but a fool
To love himself. Were there not maids enough?
The Two Noble Kinsmen

1

2

3

4

. . . all prisoners, sir,
In the line-grove which weather-fends your cell;
Ariel – *The Tempest*

5

6

7

8

9

10

11

There's fennel for you, and columbines:
there's rue for you: and here's some for me:
we may call it herb of grace o' Sundays:
Ophelia – *Hamlet*

12

13

14

15

16

17

18

Get ye all three into the box-tree:
Maria – *Twelfth Night*

19

20

21

22

23

24

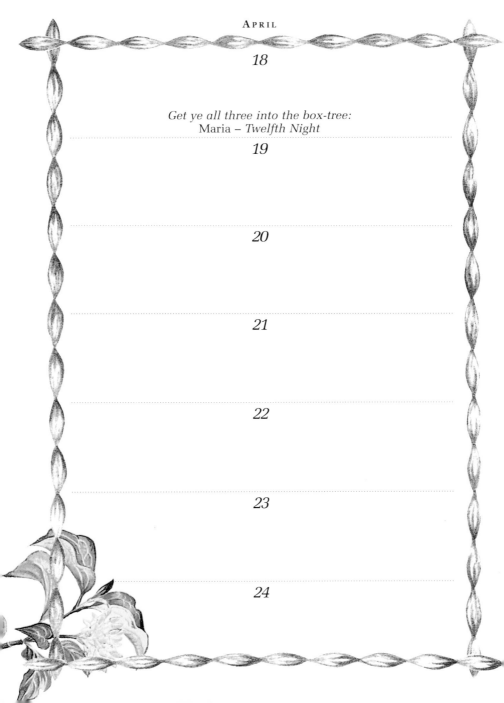

25

26

27

28

29

30

Thy banks with pioned and twilled brims,
Which spongy April at they hest betrims,
To make cold numphs chaste crowns;
Iris – *The Tempest*

MAY

. . . those lily hands
Tremble, like aspen leaves, upon a lute.
Marcus – *Titus Andronicus*

•

How like Eve's apple does thy beauty grow,
If thy sweet vertue answer not thy show?
Sonnet XCIII

•

I stamp this kiss upon thy currant lips
Thesius – *The Two Noble Kinsmen*

1

2

3

4

A wreath of bullrush rounded;
Wooer – *The Two Noble Kinsmen*

5

6

7

8

9

10

11

And here I prophesy: this brawl to-day,
Grown to this faction in the Temple-garden,
Shall send between the red rose and the white
A thousand souls to death and deadly night.
Earl of Warwick – *Henry VI*

12

13

14

15

16

17

18

So doth the woodbine the sweet honeysuckle
Gently entwist; the female ivy so
Enrings the barky fingers of the elm.
Titania – *A Midsummer-Night's Dream*

19

20

21

22

23

24

25

There's rosemary, that's for remembrance:
pray you, love, remember: and there is pansies,
that's for thoughts.
Ophelia – *Hamlet*

26

27

28

29

30

31

JUNE

*What's in a name? that which we call a rose
By any other name would smell as sweet;*
Juliet – *Romeo and Juliet*

•

*The roses fearfully on thorns did stand,
One blushing shame, another white despair;
And to his robbery had annex'd thy breath;
A third, nor red nor white, had stol'n of both,*
Sonnet XCIX

•

1

2

3

4

But hateful docks, rough thistles, kecksies, burs,
Losing both beauty and utility.
Duke of Burgundy – *Henry V*

5

6

7

8

9

10

11

And let the stinking elder, grief, untwine
His perishing root with the increasing vine!
Arviragus – *Cymbeline*

12

13

14

15

16

17

18

I know a bank where . . . oxlips and the nodding violet grows;
Quite over-canopied with luscious woodbine,
With sweet musk-roses, and with eglantine:
Oberon – *A Midsummer Night's Dream*

19

20

21

22

23

24

25

what sayest thou, my fair flower-de-luce?
King Henry – *Henry V*

26

27

28

29

30

Notes

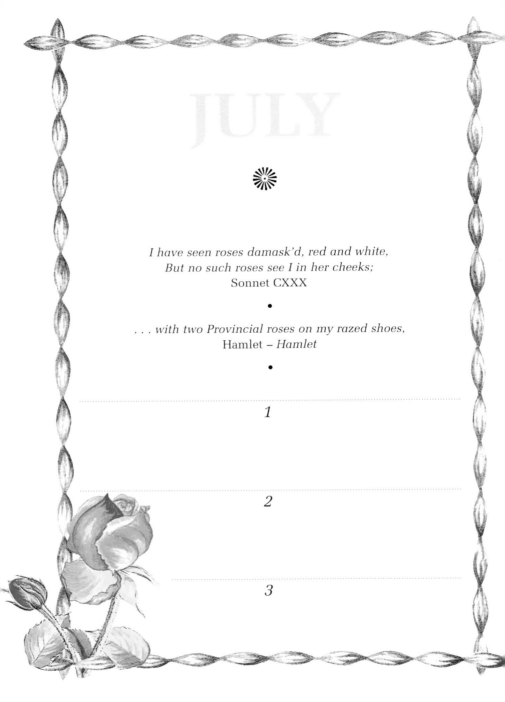

JULY

I have seen roses damask'd, red and white,
But no such roses see I in her cheeks;
Sonnet CXXX

•

. . . with two Provincial roses on my razed shoes,
Hamlet – *Hamlet*

•

1

2

3

4

Now by my maiden honour yet as pure
As the unsullied lily I protest,
Princess of France – *Love's Labour's Lost*

5

6

7

8

9

10

11

And beauty that the tyrant oft reclaims
Shall to my flaming wrath be oil and flax.
Young Clifford – *Henry VI*

12

13

14

15

16

17

18

lilies of all kinds,
Perdita – *The Winter's Tale*

19

20

21

22

23

24

25

*the fairest flowers o' the season
Are our carnations and streak'd gillyvors,*
Perdita – *The Winter's Tale*

26

27

28

29

30

31

AUGUST

✻

. . . why, he was met even now
As mad as the vex'd sea; singing aloud;
Crown'd with rank fumiter and furrow-weeds,
With bur-docks, hemlock, nettles, cuckoo-flowers,
Darnel, . . .
Cordelia – *King Lear*

✻

1

2

3

4

. . . thou hemp-seed!
Mistress Quickly – *Henry IV*

5

6

7

8

9

10

11

Of all flowers,
Methinks a rose is best.
Emilia – *The Two Noble Kinsmen*

12

13

14

15

16

17

18

Ceres, most bounteous lady, thy rich leas
Of wheat, rye, barley, vetches, oats, and pease;
Iris – *The Tempest*

19

20

21

22

23

24

25

Under the cool shade of a sycamore
I thought to close mine eyes some half an hour;
Boyet – Love's Labour's Lost

26

27

28

29

30

31

SEPTEMBER

*If reasons were as
plentiful as blackberries, I would give no
man a reason upon compulsion, I.*
Falstaff – *Henry IV*

1

2

3

4

*. . . no salve in the
mail, sir: O, sir, plantain, a plain plantain!*
Costard – *Love's Labour's Lost*

5

6

7

8

9

10

11

Thy sugar'd tongue to bitter wormwood taste:
The Rape of Lucrece

12

13

14

15

16

17

18

What rhubarb, senna, or what purgative drug,
Would scour these English hence?
Macbeth – *Macbeth*

19

20

21

22

23

24

25

The cockle of rebellion, insolence, sedition,
Which we ourselves have plough'd for, sow'd and scatter'd,
Coriolanus – *Coriolanus*

26

27

28

29

30

Notes

OCTOBER

*Your date is better
in your pie and your porridge . . .*
Parolles – *All's Well That Ends Well*

1

2

3

18

Alas, I had rather be set quick i' the earth,
And bowl'd to death with turnips!
Ann Page – *The Merry Wives of Windsor*

19

20

21

22

23

24

25

And, most dear actors, eat no onions nor garlic,
for we are to utter sweet breath;
Bottom – *A Midsummer Night's Dream*

26

27

28

29

30

31

NOVEMBER

Upon my secure hour thy uncle stole,
With juice of cursed hebenon in a vial,
And in the porches of my ears did pour
The leperous distilment;
Ghost – *Hamlet*

•

Or have we eaten on the insane root
That takes the reason prisoner?
Banquo – *Macbeth*

•

1

2

3

4

*. . . when a' was naked, he was, for
all the world, like a forked radish,*
Falstaff – *Henry IV*

5

6

7

8

9

10

11

. . . what am I to buy for our sheep-shearing feast?
Three pound of sugar; five pound of currants; rice –
Clown – *The Winter's Tale*

12

13

14

15

16

17

18

To whom the heavens in thy nativity
Adjudged an olive branch and laurel crown,
Clarence – *Henry VI*

19

20

21

22

23

24

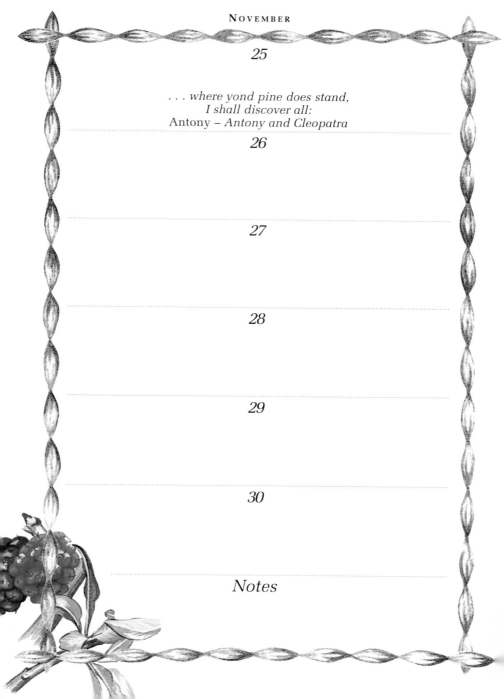

25

. . . where yond pine does stand,
I shall discover all:
Antony – *Antony and Cleopatra*

26

27

28

29

30

Notes

DECEMBER

Now would I give a thousand furlongs of sea for
an acre of barren ground, long heath, brown
furze, any thing.
Gonzalo – *The Tempest*

•

There is a man . . .
hangs odes upon hawthorns and elegies on brambles;
Rosalind – *As You Like It*

•

1

2

3

4

I must have saffron to colour the warden
pies; mace; dates, none, that's out of my note;
nutmegs, seven; a race or two of ginger . . .
Clown – *The Winter's Tale*

5

6

7

8

9

10

11

Berowne: A lemon.
Longaville: Stuck with cloves.
Love's Labour's Lost

12

13

14

15

16

17

18

Heigh-ho! sing, heigh-ho! unto the green holly:
Amiens – *As You Like It*

19

20

21

22

23

24

25

Rosalind: I'faith, his hair is of a good colour.
Celia: An excellent colour: your chesnut was ever
the only colour.
As You Like It

26

27

28

29

30

31